Praise for Other Books

by Joanna Romer

Widow: A Survival Guide for the First Year

"...a notable self-help guide that would offer knowledge, experience, and insight for others facing a similar situation. Romer's Widow is a practical compendium that covers all the critical issues a newly widowed spouse will face...Clearly the author writes from a heartfelt place. Her words stem not merely from a sympathetic point of view, but seem more suggestive of a desire to share wisdom...Ideally readers will come away from this work considering the author and her survival guide as significant new friends."

-Carol Davala, U.S. Review of Books

"Having this book by my bedside has been such a comfort. It's not the type of book you just read once and put away. No, I reach for it time and time again as new situations come up or just to reassure myself that what I'm feeling is normal."

-The Daytona Beach News-Journal

"*Widow: A Survival Guide for the First Year* is a self-help and inspirational guide for those who are coping with the loss of a soulmate. Advising how to best cope with the emotional overload, dealing with practical matters, such as the leftovers of physical possession, and most importantly, finding the way to keep living life when it seems like the last thing you want to do. Widow is a powerful and much recommended addition to self-help collections."

-Reviewer's Choice, Midwest Book Review

"Joanna Romer knows just what to say in 48 short chapters addressed to women who are accustomed to thinking of themselves as wives, but who now must learn what it means to live as another "w" word, widow. Any widow could benefit from reading this book."

-John F. Gaines, Library Thing Early Reviewers

"Written in an easy, practical style, *Widow* is a wonderful resource for anyone who has lost a spouse."

-The Villager

THE WIDOWER'S GUIDE TO A NEW LIFE

"Romer's voice is practical, experienced, and straightforward. Her advice is compassionate and upbeat but not sugary...The book is logical and clear, structured with a mix of advice and personal accounts in each chapter, progressing from one general topic to another...The scope of experience provides an overall view of what is common in grief and what is useful in recovery. The widower often needs direction, and The *Widower's Guide* is all about empowering the grieving with the hope and practical means to find a new life."

-Jason Henninger, Foreword Reviews

"Romer (*Widow*) offers consolation and encouragement to men who've lost their wives. To do this, the author shares the accounts of ten bereaved men who are going through the trauma that comes with the death of a spouse...This well-researched guidebook from an author who has lived through it herself is an excellent tool for learning how to live through loss."

-Library Journal

"Exceptionally well written, organized and presented, *The Widower's Guide to a New Life* will prove to be an invaluable source of practical information and directly applicable ideas for anyone having lost a spouse. As informed and informative as it is thoughtful and thought-provoking...highly recommended for community library collection in order to make it known and available to as wide an audience as possible."

-Self-Help Selection, Midwest Book Review

"This is a book I would give as a gift to any man who has lost his spouse...Filled with lots of good advice about ways to work through the grieving process..."

-House of Prayer, Library Thing Early Reviewers

"Because Romer directs her advice specifically to men, her book has special appeal. *The Widower's Guide to a New Life* will doubtless provide solace and assistance to its target readership."

-Barbara Bamberger Scott, U.S. Review of Books

CREATIVE AGING: A BABY BOOMER'S GUIDE TO SUCCESSFUL LIVING
(co-authored with Cheryl Vassiliadis)

"*Creative Aging* covers a lot of ground...In the chapter 'Feminism and Creative Aging,' for example, Romer discusses the fact that the women's movement initiated by boomers in their youth has had a lasting effect...In a charming chapter titled 'Is Anything Too Young for Us?' or 'Is There Anything We're Too Old to Do?' Romer makes a solid case for pursuing youthful activities and living a life unencumbered by age. Vassiliadis and Romer have crafted a book with a strong voice and a thematic approach that is just different enough to make it stand out from the glut of books targeting retiring boomers. For those who want to make the most of their later years, *Creative Aging* is a very useful guide."

-Barry Silverstein, Foreword Reviews

"In *Creative Aging*, Cheryl Vassiliadis and Joanna Romer look at how the Baby Boomer generation can go on being the creative generation that helped change the world. This is not a book that shies away from talking about the things that made this generation famous. One of the chapters is 'Feminism and Creative Aging' and another is 'Facing Death Creatively'. This is an excellent book for good answers to troubling questions."

-Library Thing Early Reviewers

"This is a wonderfully simple, yet insightful, look into aging... The chapter on feminism is truly unique and valuable. A nice guide to remaining healthy and continuing to learn new ways of healing techniques for those of us on a creative path of aging."

-Carol Anderson, U.S. Review of Books

"This timely book...is geared to help those who are at or nearing retirement creatively to plan for the upcoming years...More than a how to, this is a book that opens readers' minds to possibilities ahead. Uplifting...thought provoking."

-Deborah Bigelow, Library Journal

DIVORCED! SURVIVAL TECHNIQUES

FOR SINGLES OVER FORTY

"...a pocket companion that provides comfort and words of wisdom to help divorcees navigate the beginnings of their new lives. Divorcees may find solace in reading the many personal stories sprinkled throughout Romer's book. Readers may feel as though they're listening to a close confidante...plenty of sage advice for individuals from all walks of life."

-Jacquelyn Gilchrist, U.S. Review of Books

"I believe this is a good book for those men or women who are older and find themselves divorced or facing or even contemplating divorce. This book provides encouragement by mixing advice with real life stories from those that have gone through divorce and came out better than before. This is a smaller book and a quick read. The author touches on important areas of self-encouragement. Regaining self-esteem, using prayer and learning to live alone. I would definitely recommend this book for anyone facing the reality of divorce."

-Real Big Cat, Library Thing, Early Reviewers

"Romer writes another book full of practical advice and personal insight--with her trademark jargon-free writing style. The combination of guidelines for the newly single over forty and interviews with both men and women who have rebuilt their life after divorce offers hope. And since each new stage of life brings a sense of loss and grief (Romer has also written about the death of her husband and aging), this book speaks to a wide audience with the compassion found in Romer's other books."

-Dr. Denise Sutton, Amazon

Helping the Disabled Veteran

How to Assist Your Disabled Veteran's Adjustment to Civilian Life

Joanna Romer

published posthumously

For information, contact
MSI Press
1760-F Airline Highway, #203
Hollister, CA 95023

Typesetting & Cover design by Carl Leaver
Cover Photo & Copyright by Shahril KHMD/ShutterStock.com
Copyediting: Mary Ann Raemisch

ISBN: 978-1-942891-78-9

For veterans, their caregivers, and others who care

Contents

Introduction

On a beautiful sunny day, I found myself sitting on a bench in the Ormond Museum Memorial Gardens, surrounded by tall palm trees and lush foliage next to a small pond dotted with water lilies. It was December 7th, Pearl Harbor Day, a fitting time to visit this park, which was founded by the City of Ormond Beach, Florida as "a living monument to creative freedom and equality of all persons, and to commemorate the service of World War II veterans who fought valiantly for that ideal." Inside the Museum there is a bronze plaque inscribed with the names of Ormond Beach residents who fought in the war, with an honor roll commemorating those who perished.

The Museum does not limit itself to veterans of World War II. On the grounds we can find a monument for local soldiers who died in World War I, and more recently, two more memorials were added—one dedicated to soldiers of the Vietnam War and another to veterans of the Korean War.

The Vietnam Memorial is especially touching. A tear came to my eye when I first saw it situated at the crossroads of the path leading across the pond and the path heading back to the Museum. The realistic sculpture features a bronze chair with a soldier's helmet resting on the seat and a pair of worn boots standing underneath. A jacket is flung over the side of the chair, with a dog tag that steals focus:

THE PRICE OF FREEDOM

A folded American flag rests on the chair next to the helmet, its raised stars clearly visible. The sculpture is by artist Gregory Johnson and is dedicated to the Veterans of the Vietnam War (1959-1975)—a note on the Museum's website emphasizes "those who never returned from the Vietnam war."

The second monument is more abstract but equally stunning. Created by artist Mark Chew, the sculpture "represents an eternal flame," according to the nearby plaque. A silvery toned steel monument of symmetrical pieces reaching toward the sky, the sculpture is dedicated to the Veterans of the Korean War (1950-1953).

My late husband, Jack, served in Korea, but not in the Korean War. He served in 1962-63, the "Vietnam era," and blessedly, he did not have to fire a gun. In fact, Jack produced the Bob Hope show for the troops during his tenure, and the Army sent him to a motion picture school afterward. It was a career he followed the rest of his life. Jack was always extremely grateful to have been given that opportunity.

My husband passed on in 2011, after a long illness during which he was fortunate enough to benefit from the services of the Veterans Administration in Daytona Beach. He was always laudatory in his remarks about the VA, and I too got to know the organization well. The VA took care of Jack in his final years—warmly, professionally and with an abundance of compassion—and I was grateful.

War memorials, the Veterans Administration, our own memories of those who served in the armed forces—these are some of the ways we honor and assist our veterans. The men and women who served in World War I, World War II, the Korean War, Vietnam, Kuwait, Afghanistan, Iraq and other wars don't always have as much support as they need. It is up to those of us who care to make a difference in their lives.

#

Part One
The Need and Who's Helping

Homeless Veterans

Drive down any major thoroughfare in a medium to large-sized city, and you're bound to see this sign at an intersection: "Homeless Veteran. Please Help." The sign is usually being wielded by a man between 20 and 70 years old, bedraggled in appearance and wearing a helpless expression on his face. Sometimes the sign says, "Will work for food," especially if the Veteran is on the younger side. Sometimes the sign bearer is disabled, with just one leg, standing on crutches or in a wheelchair.

What do we do when we see such a person? The light changes and we drive on through the intersection; or, if we're feeling charitable, we put a dollar in the outstretched cup. Sometimes if we get a look at the veteran's face, a tear may come to our eye: there's something very wrong about this situation.

The more cynical among us may posit that the whole thing is an act—that the man with the sign is just a punk out to buy drugs or scam the tourists. Maybe sometimes he is, but the truth is that there were 47,725 homeless veterans in the United States in January of 2015, according to point-in-time counts in communities across the country (National Alliance to End Homelessness). Although the number of homeless veterans has been decreasing since 2009, the less cynical among us might say that there shouldn't be any.

A veteran is a man or woman who either enlisted or was drafted to serve in the military and has now completed that military service. If the individual has had a bad experience during his or her service—say, facing traumatic situations during combat, or losing a limb or an eye—assimilating back into daily life may not be so easy. There may be psychological problems, even if the veteran has not suffered an injury or has not been traumatized. The psychological problems interfere with sleep; sometimes they disrupt the veteran's ability to hold a job. After a series of dismissals from the work force—due to absences, poor performance, moodiness or even lack of sociability on the job—the veteran finds himself or herself unable to find work.

Now what? The lucky ones move in with a family member: a brother, sister, parent, or spouse if they're married. But not all vets have family members with an extra bedroom or even a couch to spare. Next comes application to various agencies for help, but again, psychological problems can get in the way. Unless the veteran has someone to run interference and demystify the red tape, it can be a disheartening experience. Some vets simply aren't up to it.

And so, sadly, we come to the street. As troops returned from operations in Afghanistan, the face of veteran homelessness changed: it is younger, more female, and often includes heads of households. Despite this change, homeless male veterans, most typically between the ages of 51 and 61, predominate. These are the veterans who served during the Vietnam War.

During times of homelessness, the veteran's self-esteem plummets; it becomes increasingly hard to even think of finding work. Alcohol and drugs may enter the picture at this point, if they haven't before, making the situation hopeless. Basically, the veteran's heart is broken. He or she has lost the will to survive. Unless someone steps in to help, the veteran's life may be lost.

Now think about it: here is a man or woman whose only crime was to volunteer (or perhaps be drafted) to help our country fight a war. Often the person was very young when the decision was made, barely out of high school. Encouraged by signs, such as, "Join the Navy! See the world!" the young person went in with high expectations.

Whose fault is it that things didn't turn out as expected? We might say, "a stronger character would have been able to pull himself out of that depression, not succumb to the psychological problems." Many veterans do pull themselves out, despite having undergone harrowing experiences, but not all. The ones who can't or whose difficulties are so extreme that anybody facing them would be laid low—these veterans need our help.

****

One person who did respond to the call for help was William J. Wood, himself a veteran of the Vietnam war, serving in the Army as a Warrant Officer. Wood had a long association with the Vietnam Veterans of America organization, an organization seeking quality health care for veterans with disabling injuries and illnesses received during military service.

Wood's involvement with veterans didn't stop there. Along with another veteran, he founded the Veterans Incarcerated Program, which helps veterans get VA benefits, provides counseling and assists with criminal justice issues. He advocated for a local property tax levy to finance services for veterans and was successful in helping the King County Veterans and Human Services Levy, which provides additional services for veterans and their families, become a reality.

Wood's work helping veterans did not go unrecognized. In 2016, the Multi-Service Center, a non-profit organization in South King County, Washington that seeks to address poverty and homelessness, named its new 13 million dollar housing facility for veterans in his memory. The William J Wood Veterans House in Federal Way, Washington, which opened in December of 2016, offers 44 one, two and three bedroom units to veterans and their families. The project was developed in partnership with Shelter Resources Incorporated and will be furnished and eligible for rental subsides through the HUD VASH Program in collaboration with King County Housing Authority.

The project came about in response to the Multi-Service Center's work with King County veterans, who identified housing and employment assistance as being among their greatest needs. The William J Wood Veterans House not only provides housing, but also offers on-site services to assist veterans who may be having trouble re-entering the job market (Vietnam Veterans of America).

Other on-site services include case management, child advocacy, and classes in basic education, financial management, technology skills and job readiness. Veterans House amenities include on-site parking, an exercise room, community rooms, computer labs and security.

On its flyer, the William J Wood Veterans House reads: "Veterans, if you are homeless, call 877-904-8387." Residents need to be referred through the VA, but all homeless or imminently homeless veterans and their families are eligible.

****

Equally inspiring is Camp Bravo in Arizona, on Tucson's south side. Here, homeless veterans can find shelter and food, as well as some TLC, at a camp run by Veterans on Patrol.

According to Martin Marszalek, the Base Commander and Chief Medical Officer of Camp Bravo, the program's mission is to find as many homeless veterans as they can locate and bring them in (Riley).

The leaders of Camp Bravo offer a safe haven, as well as assistance with those support services so badly needed by veterans. The objectives of Camp Bravo are to transition veterans from homelessness to housing and to find the veterans the medical care they need and have been doing without.

Camp Bravo, officially known as Bravo Base, is one of several in Arizona, including Camp Alpha in Phoenix, Camp Charlie in Nogales, and Camp Delta, South of Prescott. These camps have portable toilets, donated and maintained by Diggins Environmental Services, as well as land, water, and electricity provided by HMS Fasteners. Food, clothing and other supplies are donated by the public (Riley).

There are eight rules for living at Camp Bravo, which is partially supported by donations from the public. These rules include no drugs, no alcohol, no smoking in the tents, and a requirement to help out on the base on a daily basis. All the residents of Camp Bravo have tasks assigned to them, which they are more than happy to do.

****

A one-of-a-kind VA outreach program in San Diego carries the mission to help homeless veterans to a new level. A big RV from the US Department of Veterans Affairs goes out every Friday in search of these veterans, driven by a group of seasoned social workers.

Included are professionals from Supportive Services for Veteran Families, looking for veterans who meet a housing program's requirements. The program, based on grants from the VA, will provide a deposit and the first month's rent (Steele).

Other members of the VA Homeless Outreach RV Team include the San Marcos Vet Center and Mission Viejo Vet Center, the Veterans Benefits Administration San Diego regional office, Veterans Village of San Diego, Veterans Community Services, PATH (People Assisting the Homeless), and Courage to Call.

One in ten of the veterans interviewed during the Friday outreach drive will end up with full-time housing, but ten out of ten will receive information and assistance to help them change the direction of their lives, according to the program's outreach specialist, Janelle Johnson (Steele).

The program, which began three years ago, along with other efforts to end homelessness among veterans, has led to a significant dent in the problem, with San Diego reporting a nearly one-third decline (Steele).

****

The principle of the Vietnam Veterans of America organization, with which William J Wood was so involved, was, "Never again will one generation of veterans abandon another."

Judging by the commitment of its founders to this program, and also to Camp Bravo and the VA Homeless

Outreach Team, we might add: "Never again will we, the people of the United States, abandon our veterans."

\#

JOANNA ROMER

2

Legal Help

Your son Tommy came home from Afghanistan paralyzed, and you're stymied on how to help him. He's been living with you and your husband for over a year, and a good part of that time you've been trying to get a certain benefit that would help him and your family a great deal. Unfortunately, because of a supposed "hitch" in his service record, that particular benefit does not seem to be available. Tommy says the hitch is an error—but so far you've been unable to get it removed. Is there anything you can do?

Yes, there is. Paralyzed Veterans of America is an organization that provides competent attorneys to assist in cases just like this. They have litigated hundreds of cases for veterans, helping them to get the benefits they need (Legal Services – Paralyzed Veterans of America).

Veterans have the right to appeal to the U.S. Court of Appeals for Veterans Claims if their benefits request to the Board of Veterans Appeals is denied. They can even go to the U.S. Court of Appeals for the Federal Circuit. Paralyzed Veterans of America's lawyers represent veterans in the courts on these and other pertinent issues.

The organization endeavors to advance its mission outside the courtroom by educating the public on veteran claim issues. They also work to connect attorneys with veteran law resources (Legal Services – Paralyzed Veterans of America).

For further information or to request assistance, call the legal services department of Paralyzed Veterans of America at 1-800-424-8200, or email them at LegalServices@pva.com.

#

3

PTSD

In the 2017 movie Dunkirk, a soldier is rescued from an airplane wreckage by a fishing boat. He is shocked to learn that the boat is on its way to Dunkirk to help the war effort, and he refuses to go. Instead, he flies into a rage.

"He's shell-shocked," the boat captain tells his mate. The mate asks if the solder will recover and the boat captain tells him there is no way of knowing. "He may never be the same," the captain adds ruefully.

Post traumatic stress disorder (PTSD) has replaced the term shell-shocked to describe the agitated state born by some soldiers after combat. The symptoms are:

1) Headache

2) Agitation

3) Dizziness

4) Chest pain

5) Insomnia (dhproject.org)

If your veteran is displaying one or more of these symptoms, try to get him or her to talk to you about it. You can also suggest group sessions with other veterans, meditation and/or therapy.

According to the National Center for Post Traumatic Stress Disorder, cognitive behavioral therapy (CBT) is a type of counseling that appears to be effective in treating PTSD. In cognitive therapy, the therapist works with the veteran to help him or her understand and change how he or she thinks about the trauma and its aftermath. The goal is to help the patient understand how certain thoughts about the trauma create stress and make the symptoms worse (www.brainline.org).

In the area of medication, selective serotonin reuptake inhibitors (SSRD) have proved effective (www.brainline.org).

With patience, counseling and, above all, love, you can help your veteran break through the block of PTSD and live a normal life again.

#

4

Christian Reed

"Find something you love and give it your all,
like you did the military."

Christian Reed, 25, was in the military for six years and deployed in Afghanistan from November, 2012 until 2015. Unlike many with such experiences, Chris's transition to civilian life has been successful. Currently, he is a junior at Bethune Cookman University in Florida, where he's majoring in sociology.

In addition to college, which he attends with tuition paid on the G.I. Bill, Chris co-founded a youth group in his home state of South Carolina, called "Agents of Change."

"The goal is to redefine communities, one community at a time," Chris told me. He and co-founder Jonathan Jackson travel around the state to enlighten youth about how to apply for college and take steps to better their lives.

"I think Chris has a lot of confidence because of his military experience," said Dr. Paula McKenzie, an Associate Professor at Bethune Cookman University and Chris' speech teacher. "Chris is committed to making a difference in the world. He works with young people and shares his confidence."

Chris, who was stationed at Ft. Bragg where he served as Transportation Coordinator and also went to West Point to train as a commissioned officer, feels he himself has been fortunate in his transition to civilian life, partly because of his family. He has a mother and brothers in South Carolina and was able to talk to them about his experiences.

But he admits that not all veterans are as blessed in this area, mentioning friends who experienced depression and a feeling of "not being themselves."

"They had a feeling that nobody was out there for them," he explained.

Chris recommends counseling for veterans as they begin to transition out of the military, preferably twice a week.

"The information—names, addresses, phone numbers—of counselors is included in your transition packet," he told me. "They give you that but not everyone takes advantage of it."

Between school and Agents of Change, Chris does not have many hours to spare. "I lift weights, hang out with friends, and do music," he said, when asked how he spent his free time.

His advice for veterans who may be having a difficult time adjusting to civilian life:

"Find something that you love and give it your all," he says, "like you did the military."

Suggestions for Veterans

If you are having trouble with transitioning to civilian life, see a counselor. Information on counselors is available in the transition packet provided upon discharge.

Take advantage of benefits that can impact your life, as Chris did when applying for full college tuition on the G.I. Bill.

Identify something you love doing and throw yourself into it!

JOANNA ROMER

For the Disabled Veteran: Developing a Purpose

One of the hardest things to accomplish for any person facing hardship is finding meaning in life. Of course, there is the struggle to improve one's physical and mental condition, which in itself provides meaning. But sometimes there isn't a lot that can be done in this area, or if there are steps to take, the process is agonizingly slow. Meanwhile, you're frustrated, bored and feeling generally useless in terms of contributing to your family and even to yourself.

This is not a place you want to stay for long. Even though the prospect seems daunting, you will be better off if you can find something that gives purpose to your life. Many veterans find solace in helping others cope with difficulties—after all, you know what it's like to face a hardship. Veteran Chris Reed found that helping other young people better their lives through his organization, Agents of Change, gave meaning to his own life. Talking to other veterans, teaching skills to children, or even reading to the elderly in hospitals can give your life a purpose if you are compassionately inclined.

If these suggestions do not appeal to you, then look around. What sort of activities do you enjoy that could be expanded into a hobby and more? Baseball cards, stamps, rock and roll memorabilia—all can become worthwhile pursuits if you enjoy collecting, and can even bring you cash. Do you like nature? How about starting a flower or vegetable garden—even if you can't do all the work yourself, you can probably enlist the aid of a loved one to help out. The fruits (and vegetables) of such a pursuit can be enjoyed by all.

Do you have an artistic bent? Now is the time to turn that interest into a full-fledged pursuit. Try some watercolors, or write a poem. Buy some clay and try your hand at modeling, or pick up a camera and shoot some pictures (even a cell phone camera will do). Treat your ear to some classical music or vintage jazz—even if you don't play an instrument yourself, your love of the art can blossom into an engrossing passion.

You may be handicapped, but you are still a person with interests, loves and curiosity. Make a list of every single thing you've ever done in your life that you've enjoyed: watching football, playing football, reading, bowling, skiing, playing the guitar, cooking, surfing the web, surfing in the ocean, camping, horseback riding, card games, car racing, meditation, carpentry, baking pies, raising your puppy, raising your children, watching movies, making movies, gardening, rock climbing, antique car shows, antique shopping, miniature golf—the list is endless. Now narrow your list down to the activities you can enjoy now, even if only as a spectator. Spectator sports are passions for many people, and there's nothing wrong with becoming a "fan." Next, put a star by those items that could be expanded to include others in some way. For instance, playing the guitar could include teaching young people to play, composing, performing, recording and more. Cooking could include donating your famous brownies to the Veterans Day bake sale, making a holiday dinner for your family, or even writing a cook book.

You'll find that as you start thinking of ideas, your spirits will lift and more suggestions will follow. Soon you'll have a plan, and before long you'll be taking steps to put that plan into practice. This is what's known as "developing a purpose."

#

The Arts

Are you artistically inclined? Colleges, museums and community centers across the country are offering programs specifically aimed at veterans, in an attempt to provide not only art instruction but fellowship to veteran artists and would-be artists.

One such program is offered at the Southeast Museum of Photography in Daytona Beach, Florida, which is part of Daytona State College, a four-year institution. Classes are scheduled on a monthly basis for a period of nine months. The sessions allow veterans to become acquainted with professional artists in the area, as well as helping them build and enhance their own talents. According the program's website, the project hopes to help veterans "transform their experiences through the thoughtful and therapeutic form of self-expression" (Art in Action).

The classes are free and veterans need have no prior artistic experience in order to join. Participants will be given art materials at no charge. Veterans will have the chance to explore expressive painting, traditional as well as digital photography, woodcarving and decorative pottery. As each new medium is introduced, participants will have the chance to create and finish their own work of art. At the end of the program, veteran artists will have a chance to display their work in a gallery exhibition at the Museum (Art in Action).

Art in Action is the brainchild of artist Christina Katsolis, the lead technician at the Southeast Museum of Photography. The two-hour classes are open to all veterans in the community.

Guitars for Vets is a federally registered non-profit organization dedicated to helping veterans through music. According to its website (guitarsforvets.org), the organization enriches the lives of those veterans who have been injured or are otherwise struggling by providing lessons and guitars to vets free of charge. Guitars for Vets has thus far provided over 25,000 lessons and given away more than 2,500 guitars to veterans.

With over 60 chapters in 30 states, the aim, according to its website, is to restore "feelings of joy and purpose" to veterans. Guitars for Vets is administered through the Department of Veterans Affairs along with community based medical centers (Young).

7

For the Disabled Veteran:
Self-Esteem

If you are a veteran who is having difficulty re-entering civilian life, either because of a disability or simply due to a lack of opportunity, you're probably beginning to suffer from low self-esteem. No matter how successful you were before going to war, how many football trophies you won or how well you did in business, an unexpected disability can wreak havoc with your sense of self-worth. Even if you were rewarded for bravery on the battlefield, the fact that now you've lost an eye, or an arm, or are confined to a wheelchair, tends to smother that accomplishment, unless you continually remind yourself of how well you did before—and you should remind yourself, often. That's one of the ways you can recover that valuable yet fragile commodity, self- esteem, which is so important in your overall integration into civilian life.

How do we nurture our self-worth until it becomes a part of us again? By paying attention to that very word—nurture—and all its ramifications. To nurture means to go out of your way to make yourself feel cared for, pampered and loved. For instance, if you used to like to cook, and you're dying for some of your own homemade spaghetti with meat sauce, ask your wife, husband, sister, brother or whomever is your care giver to help you in the kitchen. Perhaps that person can do the shopping for you, since going to the grocery store can become a hassle. When your groceries arrive, you can start right in chopping onions and garlic, a task you used to love. Take your time, asking for help whenever necessary, but allow yourself to achieve that goal. You will feel nurtured in more ways than one.

Another example: suppose you're a hockey fan but no one else in the family is. There's only one TV in the house and four people vying to watch it—as the disabled uncle, you're probably last on the list. You know for a fact there's a sports bar in town that features all the hockey games (the owner is a fan). You can't drive, but your nephew will take you—he's even expressed a slight interest in hockey himself. Don't feel guilty about asking, and by all means don't tell yourself it's too much trouble—you'll settle for football. You owe it to yourself to figure out a way to get what you want and need. This is how we self-nurture.

Self-nurturing depends in large part on figuring out what it really is you do want, not always an easy task. Sometimes our desires are buried, particularly if we've undergone a period of heavy stress or deprivation. Try meditating or making lists of things you like in order to reactivate your desires. After you've identified some of your desires, take steps to achieve them. By turning this loving care on yourself, your self-esteem will slowly rise. If you think you're important enough to make such efforts, you must be a person of worth, right? Don't forget to reward yourself for each new accomplishment you've introduced into your life: a hot bath after a session on the exercise bike, a basket of onion rings to go with your beer at the sports bar. That's double love!

As self-esteem returns, it will become easier and easier to plan your life to include things that make you feel good. Go out for a coffee at Starbucks instead of heading straight home after work. Sit in your backyard enjoying the sunshine rather than holing up in your room, feeling blue. Ask your caregiver to drive you out to the country, or along the shore—he or she may enjoy this as much as you do.

Once you begin to cultivate self-esteem, you'll be surprised how much easier it is to do those things you have to do: applying for benefits from the VA, for example, or looking for a job. You think you're a valuable person—of course you should be treated well.

(It goes without saying that if you're a caregiver reading this book, you can apply these same suggestions for your beloved veteran. With two of you working on self-esteem, the challenge will be that much easier!)

#

Veterans Day

Veterans Day is a traditional and much needed holiday where we Americans honor our veterans in ways large and small to show that yes, we are grateful for their enormous contributions and sacrifices.

On Veterans Day 2017, one of my favorite cafes, Panera Bread, offered a free "You Pick Two" lunch special to all veterans. This is no small thing. Panera boasts some of the best and most healthful food around, and the lunch special being offered runs between $10-$13. I decided to go and see how successful this generous offer would be and enjoy my own lunch in remembrance of my husband, Jack.

When I got to Panera it was almost 2 pm, but the line stretched out the door. Of course, not everyone was a veteran. There was the usual abundance of shoppers and babies in strollers, as well as older people on a budget, but there was also a plethora of army and navy T-shirts and caps, and a sense of camaraderie that I attributed to the spirit of giving fostered by Panera.

Ahead of me in line, a young woman in jeans and a T-shirt pondered the menu on the wall. She looked uncertain. Perhaps she hadn't been here before. After identifying herself as a veteran, she ordered Autumn squash soup (my particular favorite) and a roasted turkey and avocado BLT with chips, all to go. She looked hungry, but then, so was I.

Eating my soup, I felt blessed to be in a country where merchants take it upon themselves to honor members of the military with a free meal. I remembered the last Veterans Day I celebrated with my husband, Jack, in 2010. We went to a waterfront pub giving discounts on food and drink to veterans and sat outside. It was chilly, but Jack wanted to sit at the bar and look at the boats. He sat at the end of the counter. Facing him catty corner was another man who quickly identified himself as a veteran. He and my husband launched into a fine conversation while I sat contentedly on the other side of Jack, happy that he could have this holiday contact.

Six weeks later, Jack passed on. Let's remember, as we honor our veterans, that we may not have them around forever, but at least we have them with us today.

#

Veterans at Standing Rock

Two thousand plus veteran volunteers traveled to Standing Rock, North Dakota on December 4, 2016 to protest the Dakota Access Pipeline.

Under the banner, "Veterans Stand for Standing Rock," the organizers hoped to prevent progress on the pipeline, as well as raise national awareness on the issue (Lewis).

On December 5th, 2016, the US Army Corps of Engineers announced they would find an alternate route for the pipeline. Perhaps they were influenced by the veterans, who, after all, were their brothers and sisters when it came right down to it. The victory was short-lived, as newly inaugurated US President Donald Trump signed an executive order in February to continue construction of the pipeline (Lewis).

The camp has existed since August, and at times has housed thousands of people supporting the concerns of Sioux nations that the $3.8 billion pipeline designed to carry oil through the Dakotas and Iowa to a shipping point in Illinois threatens the environment and sacred sites. The Dallas-based developer, Energy Transfer Partners, disputes these claims (Nicholson). As of this writing, the Veterans Stand group is preparing a second "deployment" to Standing Rock and have raised $186,767 to do so, according to the group's "GoFundMe" page.

"It is unlikely that we will send a mass group of people like before," said Michel Wood Jr, founder of Veterans Stand. "The biggest misconception is that Veterans Stand wants to do anything aggressive...we just want to give people a platform" (Lewis).

#

10

Veterans Memorial Park, Sanford, Florida

I'm here at Veterans Memorial Park in Sanford, Florida on a beautiful day—soft sunshine, temps about 70 degrees. The park was built in 1924 and dedicated in 1927 as a memorial to the fallen soldiers of World War I. In 1973, it was rededicated to all veterans. (Perhaps the founders were loath to be specific about adding just World War II, the Korean War and the war in Vietnam, fearing there would be more to come. How wise they were.) The park was renovated and rededicated to all veterans in 2006, and now stands as a stunning tribute overlooking the magnificent Lake Monroe, with walkways adorned with royal palms. Circling the grassy square that forms the middle of the park are hundreds or concrete tiles bearing the names of men and women who perished in war, for example:

Jerry Costa
US Marines
Semper Fi

James L. Keating
US Army
World War II
1943-1945

Constance V. Davis
US Army SFC
"Cable Dawg"
1991-2015

Korean War Vets
Brevard Co. 210
Chap Forgotten
War Remembered

There are also a number of empty tiles available, a poignant inclusion reminding us that yes, there probably will be more war deaths to come.

At the entrance of the park stands a stone monument. It reads:

NAVY
M. W. Lovell
Dedicated to the brave sons of
Seminole County who laid their lives on the
Sacrificial alter of
DEMOCRACY
In the World War
1914-1918

The park is beautifully maintained and, on this gorgeous day, well populated with folks walking around, sitting on benches gazing at the blue water of Lake Monroe, and even fishing down at the end. An American flag waves benignly in the breeze.

Looking out at the lake, where a small sailboat lazily traverses the water in almost reverential silence, I wonder how the war dead like being here. Possibly it's prettier than the homes some of them grew up in. Of course, they're not really here—only their names are, and, hopefully, their memories.

At the focal point of the park, almost at the water's edge, there is a huge monument in black marble with an eagle on top, its wings outstretched for take-off.

On one side of the monument it reads:

"A nation united can never be conquered."

-Thomas Jefferson

On the second side:

"We hereby resolve that these dead shall not have died in vain."

-Abraham Lincoln

On the third:

"Give me liberty or give me death."

-Patrick Henry

And on the fourth side, facing the lake:

"Ask not what your country can do for you, ask what you can do for your country."

-John F. Kennedy

Maybe it's because this last sentiment is so well known, or perhaps because it brings back my own youth in a way the others don't—whatever the reason, a lump comes to my throat reading Kennedy's words. How idealistic we were in the early 1960s! Can it ever be that way again?

Standing by the monument, I have a 360 degree perspective of the area—three parts water and one part downtown Sanford. It is truly lovely and inspiring.

As I turn to leave, I pass several monuments by the flagpole that I hadn't noticed before. One is dedicated by the City of Sanford to "her sons who made the supreme sacrifice in the World War," AD 1920. Another is to the members of the community, "whose generous donations helped make this park possible." There is a monument for the US Navy Enlisted Bombardier navigator, and then:

"Memorial Park dedicated 1973 to all veterans
Who have served their country well."
-City of Sanford

The fifth monument in the group under the flagpole is blank. Again, I admire the founders' realistic forethought. We are not done with our wars, it seems.

#

Part Two
What You Can
Do for Your Veteran

JOANNA ROMER

11

How Friends & Family Can Help: Running Interference

Your brother Ronnie has come home from active duty and he's a little "off." You can't quite put your finger on it, but he's just not the same person who left 18 months ago. You know he's had some rough times—he was in Afghanistan—but he doesn't want to talk about it.

If that weren't enough, he can't seem to get a job. He's living with you and your husband temporarily until he can get himself situated, but that doesn't seem to be happening. Lately, he doesn't even want to get out of bed.

You've suggested that he call the V.A., or a local group that counsels veterans, but Ronnie isn't interested. Your dear brother is hurting and he doesn't seem to know how to help himself. Is there anything you can do?

Of course there is. It could be that the very thought of dealing with agencies like the V.A. is just too much for him right now. He'd like to do it—he doesn't want to be a burden to you—but the idea of filling out paperwork in an office sends him almost to the panic point. There's no specific reason for this—and yet there's every reason in the world. War. Depression. The inability to forget what happened "over there." Post traumatic stress disorder (PTSD).

What you can do is run interference for your brother with whatever agency red tape has to be dealt with. It could be making phone calls, it could be filling out forms. It could be individual meetings to determine eligibility for a course of treatment. Whatever it is that is scaring your loved one into inertia, you can help by getting involved in a simple way to make it just a little bit easier.

He or she may not want your help at first. Pride may rear its head and try to push you away. "I'll take care of it," the veteran says—after all, this is nothing compared to what he's been through. But if time goes on and he doesn't take care of it, and you see the lethargy and depression deepen, it may be time for you to step in and help. Pick up the phone and call the V.A. Explain the situation. You need a counselor, maybe some medication—you'll bring him over yourself.

So, you go in and tell your brother you've made an appointment for him and you will go with him. To your surprise, he looks relieved. You keep the appointment. You help him fill out the paperwork (or do it yourself). You follow up with the medication at the pharmacy counter. This continues—you explore other options: a veteran's group therapy session you've heard about or a counselor in another city. Yes, it's a bit of work, but it's better than watching your brother turn into a vegetable.

Is he grateful? He may not express it to you—but perhaps you'll hear his thanks expressed in a unique way. When my late husband Jack, a veteran from the Vietnam era, went in for major surgery (not war related), I took a leave of absence from my job and cared for him night and day for two months. When we met with his V.A. doctor, Dr.

Feigenbaum, the good doctor asked Jack about his mental state. Was he depressed? Anxious?

"No," my husband declared quickly, "I'm fine because my wife stood by me the whole time. She took care of everything."

Running interference for a loved one, whether wounded, psychologically impaired, or just plain "down," requires a bit of patience as well as perseverance. Most of all it requires love—and that's something you've got, isn't it?!

GUIDELINES FOR RUNNING INTERFERENCE

1) Make those important telephone calls yourself! If you see your veteran is having trouble calling the V.A., or a veterans support group, pitch in and give him or her a hand.

2) Go with your veteran on his/her appointments to the V.A. and other agencies so you can help fill out the paperwork. If your veteran throws up his hands at the amount of red tape involved, fill out the paperwork yourself.

3) Volunteer to accompany your veteran on meetings with doctors, benefits personnel, and others who can help. If he/she says no, don't insist, but don't be surprised if your veteran is grateful for your support!

#

12

Love Heals

In the 2017 movie, "Megan Leavey," a female Marine volunteers to train an aggressive German Shepherd to be a bomb-sniffing dog in Iraq. When both Megan and her dog are injured by an undetected explosive device, they go ahead with their mission anyway, ultimately detecting explosives that would have annihilated their unit. For her heroism, Megan is awarded the Purple Heart, and both she and Rex are honored at New York's Yankee Stadium in this touching, true story.

The real story is the love that develops between Megan and her dog, Rex, during their work together. The two inspire each other to greater courage and responsibility toward their colleagues. The movie also shows some of the horrors of war, including its after-effects on the soldiers. Megan suffers from PTSD and isolates herself after her release from the Marines. It is only when she is allowed to adopt Rex as her own that she begins to start living again. It is the love that she and her dog share that heals her.

Of all the things we can give to our veterans, love has to be at the top of the list, but it has to be the right kind of love. What we give our veterans has to be something they want and need—not what we think they should have. In "Megan Leavey," Megan's mother gets her a small black puppy to take the place of Rex. The puppy's name is Lover Boy, and needless to say, does not meet Megan's needs. She doesn't want another dog. She wants to adopt Rex and save him from being put to sleep. After much effort on her part, her request is granted.

What kind of love are we giving our veteran? If he or she wants to go to a movie, do we insist the vet spend the afternoon outdoors? "The fresh air will be good for you."

If our loved one wants to sleep late in the morning, do we make him or her join the family for breakfast? Such demands, while they may seem logical for the vet's own good, will not help his or her healing. Only love will do that, love that is focused on the veteran's wishes, not our own.

We all know somewhere inside of us what we really need to be well. Our beloved veteran is no different in this respect, even though he or she may not be able to express it to us succinctly. We may have to intuit the veteran's desires from stray comments overheard, i.e.: "That new movie looks good," or, "The worst thing was having to get up at 4:30 every morning." Keep your loving antennae tuned to the veteran's wishes and you'll figure out how to really help—by giving a pure, unselfish, caring love.

GUIDELINES FOR LOVE

1) Give your veteran expressions of the right kind of love— something he or she really wants, not what you think your veteran should have.

2) Decipher your veteran's desires from stray comments while watching television or other activities, such as, "I really need to go shopping." These may not be random

remarks, but little hints of something your veteran would really like to do.

3) Respect your veteran's wishes on how to spend his/her day, where to go, who to see, and how to heal. We all know, intuitively, what it is we really need. That's giving love!

#

13

Coping with a Disability

If your veteran is missing a limb or an eye, or has a disability of any kind, caring for this beloved individual may be especially challenging. You want to make your veteran comfortable, yet you're at a bit of a loss on how to proceed. What can you do?

The most obvious solution is to talk with your veteran regarding how he/she wants to handle the disability in terms of mobility, meals, bathing and so forth. If your veteran is reluctant to discuss these issues with you out of modesty, embarrassment or both, you can look on the Internet for answers to such questions as, "How much exercise should an amputee engage in?" or, "What is the best way to bathe someone with a recent head wound?" You can also call a rehab center or the Veterans Administration for answers to some of your questions. Even your family doctor should have some advice—after all, veterans aren't the only ones with disabilities.

In the meantime, do a little research into the nature of the disability itself. For instance, if your veteran has lost the use of one eye, but not both, he or she may be able to carry on many familiar activities, but not all. Reading may be a challenge, but watching videos on YouTube will not. Going to the movies should be easy. You may have to drive your veteran to that movie—why not attend yourself? Driving itself can be very challenging, as peripheral vision can be affected.

By gently probing your veteran as to his or her comfort levels at a time when such communication is acceptable, you can determine how best to accommodate your veteran's needs. Never attempt to address these issues in public, even if there is an embarrassing episode, such as sudden bleeding, a fall or any other calamity. If something like this occurs, gently help your veteran regain composure by putting your arm around him or her and saying as little as possible beyond the amenities. Remember, your veteran is twice as embarrassed as you, and may be in pain as well.

By using common sense, being prepared for the unexpected mishap, and applying the Golden Rule, you can help your veteran cope with a disability in a way that will not cause unnecessary agitation or threaten his or her precious self-esteem.

GUIDELINES FOR COPING WITH A DISABILITY

1) If possible, try to talk with your veteran about how he/she would like to handle the disability in terms of bathing, meals and so forth.

2) If your veteran is reluctant to discuss these issues out of embarrassment or shyness, get on the internet and look up answers to questions such as, "How to bathe a head wound?" or, "How much exercise should an amputee have?" Do some research into the nature of the disability so that you're not just handing out personal opinions to your vet.

3) If you can't find the answer to a specific question, call the V.A. or a rehab center for help. If all else fails, call your family doctor for an educated opinion on dealing with the disability.

4) If a calamity occurs in public, don't make a scene or scold your veteran, no matter how embarrassed you are. Remember, your vet is probably twice as embarrassed and may also be in pain. Be compassionate!

#

14

Patience

"The two most powerful warriors
are patience and time."
-Leo Tolstoy*

We must have patience when helping our veteran. He or she may not snap back into civilian life as quickly as we'd like, particularly if there is a disability involved. If there is no disability, we may wonder, "What's wrong? Jim seems so listless, so uninterested in things. What can I do to help?"

What you can do is show an extreme amount of understanding toward your veteran, plus an absence of any attempt to "hurry" him or her. Some things can't be hurried, and the type of healing your veteran is involved in is two-fold. First, there is the re-orientation to everyday life without the constant threat of danger hanging overhead. Second, there is the necessity of making sense of what the individual has gone through in terms of his or her identity.

Both of these processes can be time consuming, especially for a person who wasn't particularly introspective in his or her former life. Now that individual suddenly finds him or herself thinking about life in new ways—especially if that new life involves a disability.

We may become impatient as time rolls on and our veteran sits in his/her bedroom staring out the window or watching television for hours on end. We may ask, "What's going on?" What's going on is healing in all its many manifestations—healing of mind, body and spirit. This takes time.

So don't ask a dozen questions every time your veteran requests a glass of water or a cup of coffee. Get the coffee and bestow it lovingly, as a gift between two people who know each other well. Along with the coffee, give your veteran the gift of patience. He or she will thank you for it, albeit silently, and you'll be blessed.

GUIDELINES FOR PATIENCE

Never try to "hurry" your veteran during his or her daily routine, such as bathing, meals or even getting from room to room. Remember, not only may your veteran be dealing with a disability, he/she is also dealing with a whole new lifestyle that needs getting used to.

Don't ask a boatload of questions every time your veteran makes a simple request, such as asking for a glass of water. Your veteran may not be ready to unburden him or herself about what happened during military service—he/she might just be thirsty!

Allow your veteran the necessary time to just sit and think about his or her new lifestyle and all that's happened, without your interference. This is called the gift of patience.

#

15

Communication

Communication is a subject that is getting short shrift these days, with all the emphasis placed on social media. Yet we as human beings need to communicate in order to be healthy—it is part of our nature. Even if your veteran is reluctant to talk, there are ways to communicate with him or her that you can explore, and you should make every effort to do this.

Yes, trying to communicate with someone who doesn't want to talk can be a challenge, but after just a few weeks of living with this individual, you will probably develop intuitive signals to help you communicate. These can include a nodding of the head, a smile when he/she realizes you understand, a hand gesture to let you know where to put the dinner tray, or a gesture to be still if you've interrupted a favorite TV show with your question.

The thing to remember with communication is that the goal is a meeting of the minds, an understanding. It is not simply that you get your message said. In fact, if you express yourself with irritation or impatience, your veteran may feign misunderstanding even if he/she does get the point.

Communication must start with an emphasis on the listener—your veteran—if you desire to get your message across. How will he or she best accept your suggestion—as a question? A humorous remark? An example from your own life? Such considerations may seem like extra effort at first, when all you want to say is, "Did you look at the want ads today?" But if your veteran automatically puts up a mental block at such a question, you have no communication. You just have words.

Take the time and trouble to get to know your veteran's communication preferences. Is he/she willing to talk a bit after a good dinner, but not before breakfast? Then don't pump him or her for information first thing in the morning. Does your veteran ask for your help in a round about way, such as inquiring if anyone needs errands done in the village before actually asking for the use of the car? Don't make things hard for him/her by playing dumb and saying, "No, there are no errands today." Make up an errand or simply offer the use of your car!

Remember, the more you can assist your veteran in communication over little things, the more he or she will trust you with information about big things—such as relationships, health, or hopes for the future.

GUIDELINES FOR COMMUNICATION

1) If your veteran doesn't want to talk to you, study his/her body language for ways to communication with him/her. For instance, if your veteran shrugs his shoulders when asked a direct question, but smiles when you phrase a request with humor, you'll know you're getting through.

2) Remember that communication is not just about getting your ideas across to your veteran. It's about his/her understanding those ideas and relating to them.

3) Keep in mind that communication starts with the listener. Take the time to figure out when your veteran is most open to talking with you. Is it after dinner? While you're preparing lunch? In the car as you do errands? The more you can adapt to your veteran's communication styles, the more successful your communication will be.

#

16

Hope

After a prolonged period of incapacity or disability, one's hope for the future can begin to diminish. Unless your veteran has strong faith, this may be true for both you and the veteran.

This does not have to be the case. Hope, and all its accompanying manifestations—such as optimism, encouragement and making plans for the future—can be nurtured.

How do we do this? The first step is to admit the possibility that things can get better. This may be hard for some, but why is it more difficult to believe this than the idea that things can get worse? After all, your veteran is alive and breathing and living with you in your home. That alone is enough to engender gratitude.

Gratitude is the key to hope, and though it may be hard at this juncture to feel gratitude, it is our responsibility to try. Sit down and make a list of everything you have to be grateful for, starting with the fact that your veteran is still alive. Continue on with your list: you have a home to share with your veteran and food to nourish him or her. If your veteran is not living with you, be grateful that he or she has a place to stay, however temporary. Be grateful for whomever is helping to care for your veteran, in whatever capacity.

Continue your list with whatever blessings come to mind: the fact that you and your veteran shared a nice breakfast this morning or had a visit from a dear friend the day before. Be grateful for the television program your veteran likes to watch, and your pet cat that provides him or her so much comfort. Be grateful for the clean sheets on your veteran's bed—you know how much your loved one appreciates that. And be grateful for the love you feel toward your veteran, a love that is returned, no matter how silently.

The door to hope opens wide when gratitude is employed, and once ajar, that door will not close. Your ongoing gratitude will keep it open.

GUIDELINES FOR HOPE

1) Admit the possibility that things can get better—maybe not necessarily on the physical plane, if a disability is permanent, but on the emotion and spiritual plane as you work together with your veteran to improve the situation.

2) Use gratitude as a vehicle for hope. Sit down and make a list of everything you have to be grateful for: ie, you have a home and food to share with your veteran.

Continue your list with small things: that your veteran has a favorite TV program to watch, and that you have clean sheets for your veteran's bed.

3) Keep the door to hope open with gratitude.

#

16

Healing Anger

As you compassionately view your veteran making his or her adjustments to civilian life, a nameless anger may simmer inside you. At first, you might not even recognize it as anger. "This is not fair," you murmur. "Barbara just wanted to serve her country and now look at her—and nobody cares!" And even, "Why do we have to have war, anyway?"

Your anger may be directed at the enemy, the military, the V.A., the government, or even God. It may be directed at yourself. Whomever is the recipient, long term grudges seldom do much good. What's needed is forgiveness—the sooner the better.

If there is something you can do to alleviate a bad situation, and your anger is motivating you to do it, by all means pursue this. But if you find yourself waking up in the middle of the night seething at nobody in particular, it is time to examine your feelings and exercise forgiveness where necessary.

Did the doctor who examined your veteran seem to rush, not spending as much time as you'd have liked talking things over? That doctor may have been overworked—forgive him or her. Did the representative at the benefits office act brusquely when you asked a question? Maybe he or she missed lunch and had answered that question 20 times that morning. Forgive that representative.

Forgive the military for putting your veteran in harm's way—after all, he or she volunteered to go. Forgive your veteran for joining the military. Forgive yourself for letting him or her go—it wasn't your decision to make.

Yes, forgive yourself for whatever infraction you think you've committed. Forgiveness is like a balm washing over your soul and cleansing it of all the pain and remorse you feel. It is the gentle hand of love acting to restore life's balance.

In the process of healing your veteran, there is no place for random anger. Instead, exercise forgiveness and let the blessings flow!

GUIDELINES FOR HEALING ANGER

1) Realize that long-term grudges, whether aimed at the enemy, the military or even yourself, seldom do much good.

2) If there is something you can do to fix a bad situation and you find your anger a motivator, feel free to pursue this. But if your anger is random and aimed at one or more nameless causes, sit down and examine your feelings. It may be time to try a little forgiveness where applicable.

3) Forgive any health professionals whom you feel have rushed your veteran through, and forgive agency representatives who may be brusque in their communication. These people quite likely are terribly overworked.

4) Forgive the military for inducting your loved one, and forgive your veteran for enlisting. Above all, forgive

yourself for everything you feel you've done wrong. It's time to start fresh, and that path begins with forgiveness.

#

18

Tact

Have you ever said something to a loved one, maybe of a critical nature, and immediately regretted your speech? We probably all have. Many times, the recipient of your remark will snap back at you with a rebuke. However, if your criticism or comment was aimed at your veteran, you may never see its hurtful effect.

It is for this reason that we should monitor our speech and avoid stray comments like, "You need to do something about your appearance—you look like something the cat dragged in." Or, "Don't just sit there like a vegetable—go out and look for a job."

Your careless simile, "like a vegetable," or, "like something the cat dragged in," may be nothing more to you than a figure of speech. To your helpless veteran, confined to a wheelchair or still reeling from PTSD, these barbs provide an extra sting to an already over-sensitive psyche.

Maybe that veteran tried to do something about his or her appearance that very morning—she applied lipstick or he washed his hair—and you haven't noticed. Your comment was based on an overall picture of a young person who is not as attractive as he or she once was. Is it necessary to berate him/her for this?

Maybe your veteran had that very day made a phone call to an employment agency. Did you bother to ask before your "vegetable" remark? I'm not saying we need to walk on eggshells around our veteran, but a simple awareness and extra tact can go far. For instance: "That's a pretty shade of lipstick, and look—I've just ironed your favorite blouse. It matches perfectly!" Or, "Dad told me you called an employment agency this morning—that's wonderful, dear." Both of these comments rely on you doing a little bit of extra work to find out what's going on or help your veteran, but in the long run, such work pays off.

Don't endlessly question your veteran for details about his or her ailment. Wait until this information is offered. Don't demand your veteran account for his or her day as if he/she is a child—there is a big difference between being wounded, whether physically or psychologically, and being a child. Don't make comments about your veteran's appearance, vitality (or lack of it), or daily activities. In fact, if you can act a little bit oblivious to everything your veteran does except things of a positive nature, so much the better. Sure, this may strike you as being unrealistic or avoiding the issue, but what is the issue here? The only real issue is healing, and your tact will go a long way toward helping your veteran bring that about.

GUIDELINES FOR TACT

1) Avoid careless remarks such as, "You need some color—you're pale as a ghost." While this may be just a figure of speech to you, the barb may sting your veteran's sensitive psyche.

2) Before criticizing your veteran, find out if he/she has actually taken action on the issue in question. Do your homework!

3) Don't compare your veteran's appearance now with how he/she used to look. The same goes for vitality—be kind.

4) Avoid treating your veteran like a child. There's a big difference between being wounded and being a child. Think how you want to be treated when you're sick, and treat your veteran the same way.

#

19

Privacy

One might think that privacy would not be an issue to an ex-soldier who has been living with dozens of other men or women with little boundaries among them. But there is a difference between the camaraderie and openness of military living, with its enforced communality, and the scrutiny your veteran may feel living at home. Privacy may become an issue without you even knowing it.

How do you respect your veteran's privacy? First and foremost, follow the Golden Rule. Ask yourself, would I want someone barging into my room without knocking—even though that person is bringing clean laundry? Chances are you would not—and neither does your veteran.

Even though your veteran may be disabled, unable to walk over to open the bedroom door or perhaps even unable see you if you do come in, he or she is not a child. You should treat your veteran at all times with the courtesy and dignity that you'd want for yourself. That means:

- Allow a private space for your veteran, even if you can't supply him or her with a room of their own.

- Allow quiet times when you do not interrupt your veteran's privacy without permission, even with food or drink.

- Allow your veteran the respect and privacy of a private phone conversation. That also means not inquiring who called—if your veteran wants to tell you, you'll be told.

- Don't pry into your veteran's emails, texts or letters "for his own good." Admit it: that's just snooping.

- Allow your veteran absolute privacy if he/she gets a visit from a friend. There is no need for you to intrude.

These things may seem obvious, but we can forget them in our desire to help and foresee our veteran's every wish or need. Remember the need for privacy is paramount and must be respected. It's only fair!

#

20

Socializing

Socializing may be a delicate issue for your veteran. Used to being surrounded by dozens of comrades at all times, where informal talk, jokes and banter were freely exchanged, your veteran may feel suddenly isolated with just two or three people in the house. He or she may profoundly miss the exchange of good will and camaraderie the military provided.

On the other hand, your veteran may want to be alone much more than you think is healthy. This may be due to shock, disorientation or even embarrassment in his or her physical appearance. Your veteran may harbor a deep desire to see old friends, but not know how to put this desire into practice.

Here's where you can step in and offer assistance. If you know your veteran would love to see her old friend Suzie, but is not sure how to initiate the contact, you can suggest a lunch at home, catered by you (but without your presence, of course). If your veteran bemoans her appearance, assure her that she looks good and Suzie will not care how her old friend looks. In fact, Suzie has called twice to inquire about getting together.

If your veteran is up to it, you can offer to drive her and her friend to a nearby café for lunch or dinner, or you can offer to cook dinner for two or three friends in your home. No, you won't be doing this every day, but socializing is important to us humans. Your veteran is no exception. You may have to break down barriers of pride, inertia or shyness to set up a social engagement, but the happiness on your veteran's face after the occasion will be worth it. The second time you do it will be much easier than the first.

If you're providing a home for your veteran in a city new to him or her, where your veteran has no old friends, make special efforts to initiate socializing. Check out the YMCA for activities your veteran might like. Investigate veteran social groups on the Internet or through the Veterans Association. You may have to do some legwork to help rebuild a social life for your veteran, but it's a task well worth undertaking.

GUIDELINES FOR SOCIALIZING

1) If you know your veteran would like to see an old friend, but feels shy about calling, suggest a lunch at home, catered by you (but without your presence).

2) Offer to drive your veteran into town to meet a friend at a restaurant for lunch or dinner.

3) If you live in a city or town that is new to your veteran, and he/she has no friends there, take the initiative to check out groups for veterans at the YMCA or V.A. Look on the internet for special activities offered to veterans, such as "Art in Action," mentioned earlier in this book. Such activities offer ways for your veteran to meet new people and socialize.

#

21

A Sense of Protection

Your veteran may need a sense of protection, and this is something you can provide with very little effort. If he or she is waking up in the middle of the night, unable to sleep, chances are there is some fear involved which the veteran may be unaware of. As a loving wife, brother, sister or parent, you can take steps to ease that fear without upsetting the veteran's efforts to re-establish self-esteem.

The first thing is to assure your veteran that you will be there for him or her. This can be done simply by saying, "You know I'm here for you. Whatever you need, just ask." You can back up these words by doing little, thoughtful things, such as making sure your veteran has access to a computer or cell phone, even if it's not for private use. Make sure, if at all possible, that their sleeping area is quiet, out of the way of household traffic, and free from pet interference. (You may be used to Rover sleeping at the foot of your bed, but to your veteran such an intrusion might be frightening.)

Try to establish regular meal times (the military is pretty good at having meals on time), and set schedules for shower use so the veteran is allowed ample time. If your veteran is disabled, he or she may need help using the bathroom or going outside; try to provide this assistance in a low key manner, without making a big deal about it. The idea is to assure your veteran that his or her needs are going to be met without having to ask or feel indebted. (You don't want your veteran to develop a sense of guilt about the extra work he or she is causing you.)

A sense of protection is essential for your veteran to feel safe and secure in his or her new environment. Remember, the new living situation is probably not something this individual ever imagined. Even if the home is familiar, the fact that the rigid protection of military rules is no long available creates a newness which must be adjusted to slowly. Treat your veteran in the same way you'd want to be treated if you were in this situation. That'll work!

GUIDELINES FOR OFFERING A SENSE OF PROTECTION

1) Assure your veteran of his/her safety in your home by simply saying, "I'm here for you. If you need anything, just ask."

2) Make sure the veteran's sleeping area is quiet and free from household traffic (including pet traffic!).

3) Set schedules for meal times and bathing so your veteran will know when these activities are available to him or her.

4) If your veteran needs help using the bathroom or going outside, provide such assistance in a low key manner, without making a big deal of it.

5) Realize that your veteran has to adjust not only to a new living situation, but a new sense of self. Be compassionate.

#

22

Encouragement, Not Nagging

Most people respond to encouragement, but it has to be done well, otherwise it sounds like nagging. Nagging is the last thing your veteran needs right now, but a little encouragement may be welcome. How can we know the difference?

First of all, encouragement is based on your veteran—on his or her needs and abilities. Nagging is most often based on you or something you'd like to see done. For instance, to tell your veteran, "That drawing is terrific! You have real talent. Would you like us to set up a little art studio for you in the garage?"—that's encouragement. To say, "That drawing is terrific! Did you follow up on those leads for art galleries I gave you? It's been over a week now..."—that's nagging.

Usually we can discern the difference by noting the usage of "I" and "you." You will usually involve encouragement; I most often falls into nagging.

The trick is to point out and praise your veteran's abilities without asking or demanding he or she do something about it. Yes, this is hard, particularly if your veteran has talent in some area and you think it is going to waste. This leads to the second major requirement for encouragement vs. nagging: time. To you, with your busy 24/7 schedule, every minute not productively used is a minute wasted. This may not be true of your veteran. He or she is in the process of healing, a process which requires time and may not always be visible. For your veteran, sitting around randomly drawing without a goal of a finished picture may be crucial to the healing process. Art, exercise, technology, cooking, writing and many other projects can lead to healing and are valuable for this purpose alone. Your veteran knows this, and that's part of why the activity is undertaken.

So if your veteran sits down at the piano and plays a little tune, applaud the effort and say, sincerely, how much you enjoyed it, but don't insist she sign up for piano lessons. If he goes into the kitchen and concocts a delicious ham, cheese, tomato and mushroom omelet, eat it with gusto, but don't demand that he become the family cook. He'll let you know when he's ready for that role.

Encourage—with love, intuition, and patience, but don't nag. Your veteran will know the difference and thank you for it.

Guidelines for Encouragement,

Not Nagging

1) Learn how to give encouragement to your veteran without nagging him to do something about it, ie, an interest in the piano or artwork.

2) Realize that "process" may be more important to your veteran's healing than meeting a goal at this time. Let your veteran dabble in watercolors, or strum the guitar, or putter around the kitchen. He/she does not have to become a gourmet chef!

3) Realize that "time" may have a different meaning for you, with your busy schedule, than for your veteran. Encourage—with love and patience—but don't demand immediate results.

#

23

Spirituality

Spirituality is more than saying prayers or taking your veteran to Church. He or she may balk at these ideas, but a spiritual approach to your veteran's healing cannot help but bless that individual.

What is meant by a spiritual approach, first and foremost, is a belief that things will improve. Having faith in the natural goodness of man and the universe, despite what your veteran has been through, will aid in healing. Your veteran has endured a lot. He or she deserves, now, to be surrounded by uplifting, positive thoughts.

Don't go around complaining about the situation your veteran is in, no matter how trying. Instead, hold him or her in your thoughts in a positive way, as healthy and getting on with life. Don't grouse about the war your veteran was involved in, or the government then or now. If your veteran complains, you can certainly commiserate, but don't dwell endlessly on negative causes or effects. Such talk helps no one and will not lead to healing.

Let your veteran exist in an atmosphere of kindness, compassion and hope. It is not necessary to preach to your veteran, maybe that's not your style anyway, but let him or her know how grateful you are to have your veteran home with you. Being grateful, having hope, expressing positive thoughts—this is the essence of true spirituality.

GUIDELINES FOR SPIRITUALITY

1) Have faith that things will get better—for you and your veteran.

2) Don't complain about the situation to your veteran, no matter how difficult. Stick to the high road!

3) Let your veteran know how grateful you are to have him or her home.

\#

24

Holidays

The holidays may be a poignant time for your veteran, perhaps more than you realize. If he or she lost a friend in battle, or simply during the course of military service, your veteran may be reminded of that friendship with sadness during the holidays. Even though you've never met this friend, you should respect your veteran's grief—the friendship may have been very close.

Your veteran may feel guilty if unable to do Christmas shopping. If they are confined to a wheelchair, for instance. You can offer to help—either by buying the items he/she picks out or by setting your veteran up on the computer to do some online shopping. It goes without saying that lending a little extra cash during this time would be welcome.

On the day of the holiday itself, don't be surprised if your veteran wants to stay in his/her room rather than join an extensive family gathering. If the need for solitude is great, don't insist on your veteran's participation in the festivities. On the other hand, if your veteran just needs a little coaxing, or maybe some help getting spruced up, by all means pitch in and accommodate him or her.

At the holiday table, relatives who haven't seen your veteran for awhile may try to ply him or her with questions. If you know this would be painful, you can ask in advance that the relative avoid this. If you see it happening anyway, be sure to jump in and change the subject—most relatives will take the hint.

If your veteran needs help eating, don't make a big deal out of this—just sit next to him or her and quietly cut up the meat or serve the vegetables. Under no circumstances should you discuss your veteran and his/her difficulties in the third person, as if he or she weren't there.

Holidays can be painful for many people—widows, widowers, parents who have lost children, and others. They can also be difficult for veterans, so be as kind and compassionate as you know how. Your veteran will appreciate it.

Guidelines for Holidays

Realize that holidays may be a time of special pain to some veterans who have lost comrades during battle.

Offer to help your veteran with activities such as Christmas shopping, or maybe a Valentine's gift for a girlfriend. You can even offer to chip in some cash if you have it.

Don't be surprised if your veteran doesn't want to join the holiday dinner table, surrounded by relatives. Don't make a big deal out of it; simply bring him/her a tray privately.

If your veteran does want to join in, offer to give him or her a hand getting dressed up.

Ask relatives in advance to avoid plying your veteran with questions during the holiday meal. If this starts to happen, jump in and change the subject.

Helping the Disabled Veteran

If your veteran needs help eating, do so quietly. By no means should you discuss your veteran's problems at the table as if he/she weren't there! Be kind.

25

Reviving the Spirit

We all know what "spirit" means—it's that energy that lends zest to our actions, that impels us to tackle each new day with enthusiasm. We can also see (or feel) when that vital spirit is lacking in our veteran. If he or she is sitting around day after day, unable to think of anything worth doing, some "spirit revival" may be necessary.

How do we accomplish this? In her groundbreaking book, Science and Health with Key to the Scriptures, author Mary Baker Eddy suggests treating the patient with "flood-tides of love" as a method of healing (Eddy). The phrase needs little translation; flood-tides of love are what we need to give our veteran in order to revive that valuable commodity.

SPIRIT.

"Flood-tides of love" implies an excess of love—not just enough caring and tenderness to get the veteran through the day, but a river of love, a torrent of love, an avalanche of love. For instance, suppose your veteran suggests going shopping. It's the first thing she's wanted to do in weeks.

Don't just go to a department store and buy a blouse or a belt or a scarf and then come right back home. Make it an excursion—find a pretty mall with a Food Court where you can treat your veteran to a yummy lunch of Chinese food or grilled hamburgers and French fries. Then go in every store your veteran suggests—you've got the time and this is important! End the shopping trip with an ice cream cone or a cup of fancy coffee and a brownie. It's not something you normally do, but your veteran will appreciate it.

Here's another example: you notice your dear veteran seems particularly interested when a pet commercial appears on television, especially one for dogs. He's never said anything about it, but one day you ask how he feels about dogs and the truth comes out. He's always wanted one. Don't let it slide. Consult with your other family members and take a trip to the Humane Society, your veteran in tow. Let him pick out the perfect pet, even though you know you'll probably be doing some of the care-taking. So what? Isn't your dear husband, sister, brother, daughter or son worth a little sacrifice on your part if it's going to restore that precious thing we call "spirit"?

Of course!

GUIDELINES FOR REVIVING THE SPIRIT

1) Surround your veteran with love, love and more love. This is the best way to revive your veteran's spirit. For example, if your veteran wants to go shopping, make it an occasion, with lunch at the food court and a coffee on the way home at Starbucks. Make it a shopping trip to remember! (It wouldn't hurt to buy your vet a small gift during shopping, like a pretty bar of soap or some shaving cream.)

2) Pay close attention to those things your veteran responds to on television, the radio or while traveling around. Does he or she seem interested in dogs? Consider getting a pet,

with the consultation of other family members of course. Would your veteran like to change his/her hairstyle? Offer a visit to a stylist, your treat. It may seem like extra work to be so attentive to your veteran's desires, but such loving gestures can pay off in the long run with a revival of spirit!

#

26

Gratitude

As we go about our daily tasks connected with taking care of our veteran, one important consideration should never be forgotten. That consideration is our gratitude that our veteran is still alive.

Yes, it is tiresome, at times, to constantly have to pick up after our veteran as if he or she were a child. Sometimes we get frustrated with our veteran's inability to speak about events that went on during his or her deployment. We may even become irritated if our veteran is less than gracious when we do something particularly nice, such as cooking a favorite meal or buying some little gift to brighten his or her day.

But remember, we're the lucky ones. We never got that onerous telegram telling us our veteran was killed in the line of duty. How grateful we are for that!

In the 1943 movie "Tender Comrade," Ginger Rogers' character, Jo Jones, receives such a telegram. She is in the middle of hosting a party for other soldiers' spouses, and she knows her husband Chris would not want her to fall apart and ruin things for everyone else. She picks herself up and calls herself a "good soldier" (her husband's name for her), as she joins the others.

That's what we need to be—good soldiers, taking care of our veteran and making sure that he or she has every comfort so well earned. Let our gratitude go with us every day that our dear veteran is still alive.

\#

Appendix

15 Ways to Help Your Veteran

1) Get your veteran a pet.

2) Take your veteran out for an ice cream cone.

3) Help your veteran fill out paperwork.

4) Drive your veteran around to do errands.

5) If he/she can drive, offer the use of your car.

6) Get your veteran a cell phone.

7) Cook your veteran's favorite meal.

8) Take your veteran to a movie of his/her choice.

9) Fix up your veteran's bed with a comforter and fresh sheets.

10) Ask your veteran what kind of music he/she likes and find a way to provide it.

11) Make the phone call your veteran doesn't want to make.

12) Help your veteran straighten up his/her room if there seems to be a difficulty.

13) Locate veterans groups and/or therapy if your veteran is interested.

14) Let your veteran use your computer.

15) Love your veteran!

THE VETERANS ADMINISTRATION (V.A.)

The Veterans Administration offers numerous benefits to veterans and their families. These include:

1) Disability compensation

2) Education and training

3) Employment services

4) Health care

5) Home loans and housing related assistance

6) Life insurance

7) Memorial benefits

8) Pension

9) Benefits to spouses, dependents and survivors

These benefits can be quite extensive. For example, veterans who have injuries, disabilities or medical conditions that were brought on or aggravated during active military service may be eligible to receive tax free monthly benefits (apply for disability compensation). These benefits are available no matter when or where the veteran served. The requirements are as follows:

- The veteran must show that he/she has a current physical or mental disability

- The disability was caused or aggravated by an injury, event or disease experienced in service

- There is a link between the veteran's current disability and the event, injury or disease in military service.

- Veterans should submit any of the following items to support their claim:

- Discharge or separation papers (the DD-214 or equivalent)

- Service treatment records
- Private medical provider records

Veterans can submit their claim online at www.eBene-fits.va.gov or by mail (Apply for Disability Compensation).

In the area of Health Care, the V.A. is second to none. In fact, the Veterans Health Administration is America's largest integrated health care system (Apply for Health Care). https://explore.va.gov/health-care

Services include:

- Access to the V.A.'s comprehensive medical benefits package, including preventive, primary and specialty care, prescriptions, mental health care, geriatrics and extended care, medical equipment and prosthetics, and more

- Most veterans qualify for cost-free health care services; some must pay a modest copay

- Women veterans can receive primary care, breast and cervical cancer screenings, prenatal care, maternity coverage, and more

For other services see https://explore.va.gov/health-care.

In the area of Employment Services, the V.A. offers benefits, resources and series to help veterans transition from service to civilian jobs and enhance their education, skills and careers (Apply for Employment Services).

For further information, see https://explore.va.gov. employmentservices.

THE SOLDIER'S PSALM

Psalm 91 has been called the Soldier's Psalm because of an unusual incident during World War I. The men in the 91st Infantry Brigade of the U.S. Expeditionary Army were all given the psalm printed on little cards right before going into battle. The 91st Brigade was engaged in three of the worst battles of the war—the Argonne, Chateau Thierry, and Belle Wood, but the men prayed the psalm daily and suffered not a single casualty. Other American units engaged in those same battles had up to 90% casualties (The Soldier's Psalm).

With such a record, it's no wonder that the psalm has become known throughout the world as providing protection for soldiers. As a veteran, perhaps you've heard of it; maybe you've even prayed it yourself. If you're a friend, sister or brother of a veteran, you may not be aware of the power of Psalm 91—perhaps now is the time to become acquainted:

Psalm 91

1   He that dwelleth in the secret place of the most High shall abide under the shadow of the Almighty.

2   I will say of the Lord, He is my refuge and my fortress: my God; in him will I trust.

3   Surely he shall deliver thee from the snare of the fowler, and from the noisome pestilence.

4   He shall cover thee with his feathers, and under his wings shalt thou trust: his truth shall be thy shield and buckler.

5   Thou shalt not be afraid for the terror by night; nor for the arrow that flieth by day;

6   Nor for the pestilence that walketh in darkness; nor for the destruction that wasteth at noonday.

7   A thousand shall fall at thy side, and ten thousand at thy right hand; but it shall not come nigh thee.

8   Only with thine eyes shalt thou behold and see the reward of the wicked.

9   Because thou hast made the Lord, which is my refuge, even the most High, thy habitation;

10 There shall no evil befall thee, neither shall any plague come nigh thy dwelling.

11 For he shall give his angels charge over thee, to keep thee in all thy ways.

12 They shall bear thee up in their hands, lest thou dash thy foot against a stone.

13 Thou shalt tread upon the lion and adder: the young lion and the dragon shalt thou trample under feet.

14 Because he hath set his love upon me, therefore will I deliver him: I will set him on high, because he hath known my name.

15 He shall call upon me, and I will answer him: I will be with him in trouble; I will deliver him, and honour him.

16 ßWith long life will I satisfy him, and show him my salvation.

❋❋❋❋❋❋❋❋❋❋❋❋❋❋❋❋❋❋❋❋❋❋❋❋❋❋❋❋❋❋

The psalm is also famous for its connection to the beloved actor, James Stewart. Stewart, who enlisted in the Air Corps and became part of a bomber squadron during World War II, was given the psalm by his father, Alexander Stewart, when he was preparing to fly overseas. James Stewart's dad came to the farewell ceremonies in Sioux City, Iowa and slipped a small envelope into his son's pocket.

That night, alone in his bunk, Stewart opened the envelope. The note from his father read: "My dear Jim, soon after you read this letter, you will be on your way to the worst sort of danger. I have had this in mind for a long time and I am very concerned...But Jim, I am banking on the enclosed copy of the 91st Psalm.

"The thing that takes the place of fear and worry is the promise in these words. I am staking my faith in these words. I feel sure God will lead you through this mad experience...I can say no more, I only continue to pray. God bless you and keep you. I love you more than I can tell you. Dad" (Guidepost Classics).

Stewart said he cried reading this note, because his dad had never said he loved him until then. He began to read the psalm and the small booklet with it, entitled "The Secret Place—A Key to the 91st Psalm." He read from the booklet before every bombing raid, and the meaning of the psalm deepened (Guidepost Classics).

Stewart returned safely from the war to make many more films, including the classic "It's a Wonderful Life." Coming home as a decorated war hero, Stewart said he learned to lean on the words of Psalm 91 (The Soldier's Psalm).

In 1969, a group of men who were members of the First Brigade of the 101st Airborne Division during the Vietnam War were trapped at a placed called Hill 376. They were outnumbered and pinned down by fierce enemy fire. These men, the only survivors of the battle, returned 30 years later to pay their respects to their fallen brothers and to seek further healing for their own hearts. One of the men took out a Bible and began to read Psalm 91.

As a veteran, you can use Psalm 91 for healing just as it was used for protection during various wars. Maybe you have nightmares about the tragedies you've seen—you can't seem to get over it. You can interpret the psalm in a new way:

"You will not be afraid of the terror by night, or of the arrow that flies by day. Or the pestilence that walketh in darkness. Or of the destruction that lays waste at noon."

These verses, which have bolstered soldiers on the battlefield, can strengthen veterans battling to recover their well-being now at home.

Your beloved son, brother or husband may feel like he is still on the battlefield. The terror is still there at night and often in the daytime as well. What you can do is pray for your loved one's peace of mind and refer to Psalm 91 for comfort. If your beloved veteran is not familiar with the psalm, he or she will be moved by the deep message of comfort and consolation it contains.

#

References

Apply for Employment Services, https://explore.va.gov.employmentservices Retrieved January 14, 2017

Apply for Health Care, https://explore.va.gov/health-care Retrieved January 14, 2017

Art in Action, Christina Katsolis, Southeast Museum of Photography, https://www.smponline.org/ Retrieved February 6, 2017

Eddy, Mary Baker, *Science and Health with Key to the Scriptures*, Christian Science Publishing Society, Boston, MA 2006

Guidepost Classics, https://www.guideposts.org Retrieved January 8, 2017

Guitars for Vets, https://www.guitars4vets.com Retrieved September 12, 2017

Legal Services, Paralyzed Veterans of America, www.pva.org/find-support/legal-services Retrieved March 2, 2017

National Alliance to End Homelessness, http://endhomelessness.org Retrieved January 8, 2017

Lewis, Sophie, CNN, "Veterans Stand for Standing Rock" November 23, 2016 Retrieved March 21, 2017

Riley, Mitchell, "Homeless veterans take refuge at Arizona encampment," PBS PBS Newshour, January 14, 2017

Steele, Jeanette, "Helping homeless veterans, one RV trip at a time," The San Diego Union-Tribune, December 9, 2016 Retrieved February 20, 2017

The Soldiers' Psalm, https://www.thoughts-about-god.com Retrieved May 2, 2017

Veterans Administration, https://explore.va.gov Retrieved January 15, 2017

Vietnam Veterans of America, https://vva.org Retrieved January 5, 2017

www.brainline.org, all about brain injury and PTSD, Retrieved February 18, 2017

Young, Pat, "Guitars for Vets", Hometown News, October 27, 2017

Letter to the Reader

Dear Reader,

Before you put down this book, may we ask for your help? Getting the word out about our books is very important to our authors. Would you be willing to help?

The best way to help is write a review of this book. You can leave the review on Amazon, Barnes & Noble, or other online bookseller site. Or on Twitter, Instagram, Face Book, etc. Or you can share it with us. (Endorsements are also welcome—please send those to the publisher, too.)

If you are a blogger and like this book or any other book by Joanna Romer, a review on your blog will really help. We can provide you with a graphic of the cover if you need that. You may contact me through my editor, editor@msipress.com.)

Also, it is with great sadness that we tell you that this is Joanna's last book (other than a co-authored book with Pat Young, *Life after Losing a Child*, that will appear in 2019). We are publishing it posthumously since she had finished it a few months before she passed away in July 2018. Her MSI Press family is diminished by her absence, and we hope that her fans will be glad to have 1-2 more books from their beloved authors.

Thank you all for your support of our press and of one of our most beloved authors,

The Staff at MSI Press

Books by Joanna Romer

Select MSI Books

SELF-HELP BOOKS

100 Tips and Tools for Managing Chronic Illness (Charnas)

A Woman's Guide to Self-Nurturing (Romer)

Care for the Catholic Caregiver (Franklin)

Creative Aging: A Baby Boomer's Guide to Successful Living (Vassiliadis & Romer)

Divorced! Survival Techniques for Singles over Forty (Romer)

How to Get Happy and Stay That Way: Practical Techniques for Putting Joy into Your Life (Romer)

How to Live from Your Heart (Hucknall) (Book of the Year Finalist)

Living Well with Chronic Illness (Charnas)

Overcoming the Odds (C. Leaver)

Publishing for Smarties: Finding a Publisher (Ham)

Recovering from Domestic Violence, Abuse, and Stalking (Romer)

Survival of the Caregiver (Snyder)

The Rose and the Sword: How to Balance Your Feminine and Masculine Energies (Bach & Hucknall)

The Widower's Guide to a New Life (Romer)(Book of the Year Finalist)

Widow: A Survival Guide for the First Year (Romer)

Widow: How to Survive (and Thrive!) in Your 2d, 3d, and 4th Years (Romer)

INSPIRATIONAL AND RELIGIOUS BOOKS

A Believer-in-Waiting's First Encounters with God (Mahlou)

A Guide to Bliss: Transforming Your Life through Mind Expansion (Tubali)

Care for the Catholic Caregiver (Franklin)

El Poder de lo Transpersonal (Ustman)

Everybody's Little Book of Everyday Prayers (MacGregor)

How to Argue with an Atheist: How to Win the Argument without Losing the Person (Brink)

Jesus Is Still Passing By (Easterling)

Joshuanism (Tosto)

Living in Blue Sky Mind: Basic Buddhist Teachings for a Happy Life (Diedrichs)

Passing On: How to Prepare Ourselves for the Afterlife (Romer)

Puertas a la Eternidad (Ustman)

Saints I know (Sula)

The Seven Wisdoms of Life: A Journey into the Chakras (Tubali) (Book of the Year Finalist)

When You're Shoved from the Right, Look to Your Left: Metaphors of Islamic Humanism (O. Imady)

Memoirs

57 Steps to Paradise: Finding Love in Midlife and Beyond (Lorenz)

Blest Atheist (Mahlou)

Forget the Goal, the Journey Counts . . . 71 Jobs Later (Stites)

From Deep Within: A Forensic and Clinical Psychologist's Journey (Lewis)

Good Blood: A Journey of Healing (Schaffer)

Healing from Incest: Intimate Conversations with My Therapist (Henderson & Emerton) (Book of the Year Finalist)

It Only Hurts When I Can't Run: One Girl's Story (Parker)

Las Historias de Mi Vida (Ustman)

Of God, Rattlesnakes, and Okra (Easterling)

Road to Damascus (E. Imady)

The Optimistic Food Addict (Fisanick)

Tucker and Me (Harvey)

FOREIGN CULTURE

Syrian Folktales (M. Imady)

The Rise and Fall of Muslim Civil Society (O. Imady)

The Subversive Utopia: Louis Kahn and the Question of National Jewish Style in Jerusalem (Sakr)

Thoughts without a Title (Henderson)

PSYCHOLOGY & PHILOSOPHY

Anger Anonymous: The Big Book on Anger Addiction (Ortman)

Anxiety Anonymous: The Big Book on Anxiety Addiction (Ortman)

Awesome Couple Communication: Expressing What You Mean and Understanding What the Other Meant (Pickett)

Depression Anonymous: The Big Book on Depression Addiction (Ortman)

Road Map to Power (Husain & Husain)

The Marriage Whisperer: How to Improve Your Relationship Overnight (Pickett) (IPPY Living Now Gold Medal)

Understanding the Analyst: Socionics in Everyday Life (Quinelle)

Understanding the Critic: Socionics in Everyday Life (Quinelle)

Understanding the Entrepreneur: Socionics in Everyday Life (Quinelle)

Understanding the People around You: An Introduction to Socionics (Filatova)

Understanding the Romantic (Quinelle)

Understanding the Seeker: Socionics in Everyday Life (Quinelle)

HUMOR

Cold Heat and Crazy Doctor (S. Leaver)

Mommy Poisoned Our House Guest (S. Leaver)

The Musings of a Carolina Yankee (Amidon)

Parenting & Teaching

365 Teacher Secrets for Parents: Fun Ways to Help Your Child in
  Elementary School (McKinley & Trombly) [Recommended by US
  Review of Books; Selected as USA Best Book Finalist]

How to Be a Good Mommy When You're Sick (Graves)

Methods of Individualization in Teaching Foreign Languages (Leaver,
  tr. Krasner)

I Am, You Are, My Kid Is... (Leaver)

Lessons of Labor (Aziz)

Understanding the Challenge of "No" for Children with Autism
  (McNeil)

Pets

Christmas at the Mission: A Cat's View of Catholic Beliefs and Customs
  (Sula)

How My Cat Made Me a Better Man (Feig) (Book of the Year Finalist)

Intrepid: Fearless Immigrant from Jordan to America (Leaver & Leaver)

Surviving Cancer, Healing People: One Cat's Story (Sula)

Tale of a Mission Cat (Sula)

CPSIA information can be obtained
at www.ICGtesting.com
Printed in the USA
LVHW041930030320
648856LV00012B/1302